C000277968

by

Chris Wright

© Chris Wright 2013
Paperback ISBN: 978-0-9927642-1-0
Also available as an e-Book ISBN: 978-0-9933941-0-2

PUBLISHED BY
WHITE TREE PUBLISHING
BRISTOL
UNITED KINGDOM

wtpbristol@gmail.com

About the Author

Chris Wright is married with three grownup children, and lives in the West Country of England where he is a home group leader with his local church. He has written many books, mostly for young readers. Here are Christian books currently in print with White Tree Publishing. Most titles are also available as e-Books in most formats.

For family reading:

Mary Jones and Her Bible: An Adventure Book
ISBN 978-0-9525-9562-5

Pilgrim's Progress: An Adventure Book ISBN 978-0-9525-9566-3

Pilgrim's Progress — Special Edition ISBN 978-0-9525-9567-0

Zephan and the Vision ISBN 978-0-9525-9569-4

Agathos, The Rocky Island, and Other Stories
ISBN 978-0-9525-9568-7

For older readers:

So, What Is a Christian? An introduction to a personal faith, a companion to this book. ISBN: 978-0-9927642-2-7

Running Through the Bible ISBN: 978-0-9927642-6-5

Starting Out – help for new Christians of all ages, a companion to this book ISBN 978-1-4839-622-0-7

English Hexapla — The Gospel of John ISBN 978-0-9525-9561-8

Many adults enjoy *Pilgrim's Progress — Special Edition*.
(ISBN 978-0-9525-9567-0.) The story sticks closely to the events in John Bunyan's book and is set in that period, but Christian and Christiana are teenagers. A painless way to become familiar with the original!
You can find further details on all these books on the websites of major internet booksellers and buy some titles from bookstores. Churches and Christian organizations worldwide can purchase multiple copies of *Starting Out*, *Help!*, *Running Through the Bible* and *So, What Is a Christian?* from the publisher.

Before We start

This book uses verses from the *New International Version*, a modern translation of the Bible. On page 25 there are examples of two other English Bible translations. It may be helpful for some readers to get an idea of different versions available, all of which are translations from the Hebrew and Greek in which the books of the Bible were originally written.

One of these translations is the *Authorized King James Version* (KJV) that goes back to 1611, and is still widely used today. We also have *The Message* (TMG), which is not so much a word-for-word translation as one that gives meaning to the original words and expressions by putting them into informal everyday language. Great for reading, but you might want a more conventional version for studying.

If you already belong to a church, you will be familiar with a Bible similar, but perhaps not identical, to one of these. Although some people may feel strongly that one version is better than another, bear in mind that they are all translations into English, letting us read what God has to say to us. We must be thankful that his Word is available to us today, in whatever version we choose.

For anyone not sure how Bible references are quoted (such as John 3:16), the first number (3 here) is the chapter of the named book (John), and the second number (16) is the verse of that chapter. The index at the front of a Bible will show you the page numbers for the start of the books. Don't be afraid to use it!

Introduction

This is a short book primarily for young people, who are starting the adventure of living the Christian life. This is probably why you're reading it. Maybe you've been brought up in a Christian family and you've now come to accept Jesus as your own Saviour — so he's no longer just the Saviour of your parents or friends. No one else could do that for you, because you needed to take that step yourself. Or perhaps you're the only Christian in your family. If so, remember that no one is on their own as a Christian. Jesus promises, "I am with you always." You can praise the Lord for that!

Don't expect to be a perfect Christian — ever! As you go on as a Christian, you'll have your ups and downs, but each step of the way should bring you closer to God. Don't forget that it is Jesus, the Good Shepherd, who looks after his sheep. You're in his hands now — the safest hands of all to be in.

How great is the love the Father has lavished on us, that we should be called children of God! And that is what we are! The reason the world does not know us is that it did not know him (1 John 3:1).

What is a Christian, anyWay?

We call God our Heavenly Father. Of course, God is the creator of everyone, but in a very special way he is the *Father* of those people who are in his family. This is what John says when he tells us about Jesus.

He came to that which was his own, but his own did not receive him. Yet to all who received him, to those who believed in his name, he gave the right to become children of God — children born not of natural descent, nor of human decision or a husband's will, but born of God (John 1: 11-13).

Think about your own family. You're part of your family because you were born or adopted into it. So to be part of God's family you must be born into God's family. You have been born first into your own family. Now the amazing bit: you've become a Christian, which means you really *have* been born into God's family! You may not understand it, but that is exactly what Jesus said must happen, so that we can get to heaven. Here is what Jesus says:

"I tell you the truth, no one can see the kingdom of God unless he is born again" (John 3:3).

So there can't be "ordinary" Christians and some sort of special "born again" Christians. To be a Christian *is* to be born again. "Saved" and "converted" are words that are sometimes used to describe how you can become a Christian. The words themselves are not important. What *is* important is that you've realised you could never get to God by yourself, but need his Son, Jesus, to help you. Perhaps you prayed something like this:

"Lord Jesus, I believe that you died on the Cross to take the punishment for my sins. Please take my sins away. I turn from everything that I know is wrong. Come and be my Saviour. Come into my life by your Holy Spirit, make me one of God's very own children, and be with me now and for ever. Thank you, Jesus. Amen.

And Jesus promises that now you are indeed in God's family, because he never lies. This is like getting a letter with the most wonderful news you could think of. And of course it *is* the most wonderful news you could get — ever!

"Are you sure?"

Who do you think asks you this question? Certainly not your Heavenly Father. He says you *can* be sure! In the Bible we read:

This righteousness from God comes through faith in Jesus Christ to all who believe. There is no difference, for all have sinned and fall short of the glory of God, and are justified freely by his grace through the redemption that came by Christ Jesus (Romans 3: 22-24).

What is Grace? When we've done wrong, Justice is getting what we deserve. Mercy is not getting what we deserve. Grace is getting something from God, because he loves us so much, that is way, way better than anything we deserve. And Justified means being made "Just-as-if-I'd" never sinned — completely free from God's judgment.

It's easy to think that God means everyone *except* you — because you don't think you deserve it — but "all" in this Bible passage means "all", so you are definitely included. God doesn't tell lies. When you realize this, you will suddenly see just how many promises there are for *you* in the Bible. So you *can* be sure. Then why does the question — "Are you sure?" — keep coming up?

Jesus found that his enemy Satan — the devil — kept bothering him. When Satan came, Jesus remembered promises in the Bible, and Satan didn't like it. He went away. Satan, the devil, is our enemy too. What Jesus did, we can do. It is Satan who says, "Are you sure?" Learn this promise from Jesus:

> "I tell you the truth, whoever hears my word and believes him who sent me has eternal life and will not be condemned; he has crossed over from death to life" (John 5:24).

You can repeat this out loud when you begin to wonder if you really have become a Christian. You see, it doesn't depend on *you*, but on *Jesus*. Jesus also says:

> "Here I am! I stand at the door and knock. If anyone hears my voice and opens the door, I will come in and eat with him, and he with me" (Revelation 3:20).

Not *might* come in, not *sometimes* come in, but *will* come in. Praise God, and thank Jesus right now that he really did come into your life when you asked him. And if you haven't asked him in, do it now before you read any further. Turn back to page 4 and you can use the prayer there.

Think for a moment about the amazing love of Jesus — he died for you. Can you see it now?

"I'm still not good enough!"

That's not surprising, because nobody is! Not even the most wonderful preacher or missionary. God knows that. That's why he sent Jesus to die for us.

> *For it is by grace you have been saved, through faith — and this not from yourselves, it is the gift of God — not by works, so that no one can boast* (Ephesians 2:8-9).

You're still not good enough for what? Not good enough to earn a place in heaven? Certainly you're not good enough for that! You don't deserve God's love. Accept the gift as a gift. No matter how bad you've been (the Bible calls it sin) God loves you.

Many new Christians worry about how much wrong there suddenly seems to be in their lives. If you're rowing a boat down a river you don't notice that the river is flowing with you. When you turn round and row back up the river, you discover just how strong the current is. When we become Christians we turn around and suddenly see the power of wrong things in our lives.

When Jesus lived on earth, he met two sorts of people. He called them the "well" and the "sick". He said it's the sick people who need the doctor, not the people who are well.

What Jesus means is that the people who think their lives are good enough won't bother to turn to him. It's the people who know they "aren't good enough" who need Jesus — and that means all of us. But only some people realise it. You can read exactly what Jesus said in Matthew chapter 9.

You've probably done some bad things that you're now ashamed of. You feel guilty. Maybe you've done some *very* bad things, and the thought of them makes you feel that there's no way God will forgive you. Well, here's some good news. We don't need to go round with long faces thinking of all the wrong things we've ever done. Praise God and thank him for making you his very own. Those wrong things are in the past.

> *If we claim to be without sin, we deceive ourselves and the truth is not in us. If we confess our sins, he is faithful and just and will forgive us our sins and purify us from all unrighteousness* (1 John 1:8-9).

But what of the things you *keep* doing wrong? You mustn't think they don't matter, even though you're forgiven. Tell God you love him, and tell him about the things you find difficult to do — or not do. Above all, tell him you're sorry and ask for forgiveness.

The verses above from 1 John were written for Christians. When you've said sorry, accept that you've been forgiven. It's a gift. You don't earn it. Don't trust your feelings. Trust God's Word. Pray that what you read and hear will go from your head to your heart.

The Bible

The Bible is the main way God teaches us about himself and about his plan for our lives. In the Bible there are promises that can come alive in a special way as God tells us they are for us today, not just for the people who lived in Bible times.

Do you have a Bible of your own? Do you read it? Within the last few years many new editions of the Bible have appeared in modern English. When the Bible was first written, it was written in the language of the Bible lands — Hebrew and Greek. It has to be translated before most of us can read it.

The best known translation into English was made in 1611. That was a long time ago, and English people used a language that some people find old fashioned. The 1611 translation is called the King James Authorized Version (KJV for short).

People who have been brought up to read the KJV are familiar with the language, and love it. People who have only read books in modern English may find the KJV difficult to understand in places. So if you think that reading the Bible won't be easy, have a look at a modern translation. Apart from the language, it's still the same book — God's Book.

As you read the Bible now that you're a Christian, it may seem a different book to you than it did once. You will read and understand things you never realized were there before! The reason is found in the Gospel of Luke where Jesus is helping his disciples:

Then he opened their minds so they could understand the Scriptures (Luke 24:45).

Jesus made blind people see, and he opens the "eyes" of our minds. He is helping you to understand the Bible, too.

If you're choosing a Bible for yourself, you may want to buy the version that your church uses — if you already belong to a church. Anyway, look at some different translations. You'll see them in Christian bookshops, ordinary bookshops, and churches. Some are printed in paperback to keep the cost low. Often you can buy just the New Testament.

The New Testament is about Jesus and the first Christians. There's a lot of advice about living the Christian life in the New Testament. Better to buy a New Testament or even a single Gospel than nothing at all; but when you can afford it, buy a complete Bible so you can read the Old Testament as well.

The Old Testament starts at the beginning of the world. It ends at a time when different Godly men tell the people to watch for a Saviour who would come to forgive their sins and open the way to God. This Saviour was, of course, Jesus.

It's exciting to see that in the New Testament we not only read about Jesus, but are told that he will be coming again; not as he did the first time, but coming to take all Christians to heaven — and that is just one of the many things you'll discover in a Bible of your own. Become a Bible bookworm for Jesus Christ!

N℮W read it!

Whichever English translation of the Bible you choose, you will need to use it. You don't use a Bible by putting it on a shelf as a dusty ornament — you use it by reading it every day. Yes, but how do you go about it?

Some people find it difficult to know where to start. The Bible is mainly a mixture of history, poetry and help on living the Christian life. If you start with Genesis chapter 1, and read right through to the end, you'll probably find much of it difficult to understand without help.

Don't delay reading the Bible. Start right away if you can. Where do you start? Turn to the four Gospels — Matthew, Mark, Luke and John. (Don't be ashamed to use the index at the front of the Bible to find them, although try to learn where they, and other books are, if you can.) The Gospels tell us about Jesus. Gospel means Good News. The Gospels of Mark and John are probably the best to start with.

Read a few verses every day. Of course, you can read more if you like! Now we come to something different. Using a pen or coloured pencil, underline or draw a circle round any verses that you feel are special to you. Special? Well, it's up to you to decide which verses you choose, but you'll soon get the idea.

It may seem strange to you, to be marking lines on a Bible — especially a new one. Remember, though, that your Bible is going to be used daily. Of course, if you have an expensive presentation Bible you can mark up a cheaper one. Choose a pen that doesn't come through the page and show on other side. If it does, the results can be extremely confusing!

When you've read the whole Gospel, you can read back over the verses you've marked. Then you can start on another book of the Bible. As you grow as a Christian, you'll probably find yourself marking verses you never even thought to mark before.

Several Christian publishers print Bible reading notes. These set out a few verses to read each day and explain them as you go, often including a short prayer. Ask at your church or Christian bookshop. With these notes, you can read through the Bible in a very interesting and helpful way.

One thing to remember: the Bible is God's Book, and he will use it to teach you, help you, and above all bring you closer to him each day. Before you read, ask him to "open your eyes". That's when God's Word really comes alive.

Still not got a Bible of your own? Does the cost of a Bible seem too much? Well, think how much you've spent recently on your clothes, sports, games and hobbies. Does a Bible seem so expensive now! But if you really can't afford a Bible, your church minister (I hope you belong to a church by now), or someone there, will lend, and maybe even give you one.

Now you need to put time aside each day to read it!

Praying

You will have prayed one important prayer already and really meant it. That was the one when you asked Jesus to come into your life. Since then, you've probably prayed all sorts of prayers.

Now, should you pray to God the Father, to Jesus, or to the Holy Spirit? Don't worry if you can't understand the difference between the three names. It *is* very difficult. God is one God, and yet he is called the Trinity. Trinity means three people in one. This book is not the place to try to explain this, but the following should help.

Pray to God the Father when you want to talk about things in the way someone might talk to their own father if they get on well together. Saying sorry, asking for things, sharing any worries, and generally talking things over.

Pray to Jesus as you would talk to a friend who is with you, a friend you would confide in with your most secret thoughts. Jesus *is* with you, even though you may not understand how.

Ask the Holy Spirit to guide you and give you power to do something for God. The Bible tells us that *the Holy Spirit is God living in us*. Isn't that amazing? Ask the Holy Spirit to fill you with power so that God can use you to work for him. Ask him right now if you haven't done so already.

Jesus said ... "You will receive power when the Holy Spirit comes on you; and you will be my witnesses ... to the ends of the earth" (Acts 1:8).

13

You don't have to be too concerned about whether you're using the right name for each prayer. There's only one God — and we know him as Father, Son and Holy Spirit. If you would rather just pray to God or Jesus, then do. You could say "Lord", which gets over the difficulty of using another name, but don't forget what "Lord" means. If you call God the Father (or Jesus) Lord, it means you're putting him *first* in your life. First — even before yourself! If doing what *God* wants is more important to you than doing what *you* want, you can say "Lord" and mean it.

To some Christians, praying only comes with practice. It may be weeks before you can pray more than a few sentences at a time. Perhaps even then only in private. Other people find it hard to stop in public! Get into the habit of praying all through the day.

The Bible tells us to "pray without ceasing". That doesn't mean you have to spend all your time on your knees! You can pray as you walk down the road, as you drive, or ride your bike, play games, and talk with your friends. All the time be aware that Jesus is living with you now. Think about that for a moment. He wants you to talk to him. You can pray out loud, or you can pray in your thoughts.

Praying is not *just* asking. However, we're told in the Bible to ask for things in prayer. Don't be greedy or selfish, but do ask for *definite* things that you believe would be in line with God's will — and praying for someone to become a Christian is very definitely in line with God's will.

If you're praying for yourself, family or friends, say exactly what you want God to do. Make a note of what you pray for, and see how God answers prayer. Many prayers are answered quickly, but you may have to wait. Of course, prayers aren't *always* answered the way you expect. But because you've prayed, you will have been brought closer to God. And when you pray, pray in Jesus' name.

When a prayer is answered, you can really praise God and thank him. If you want to thank God while you're waiting, you can thank him for *hearing* your prayers. Thanking God is easy. You can thank him for everything. Maybe you've prayed, "I ask you, Lord, for . . ." Well it's up to you to fill in the missing words, and later remember to change the word "ask" to "thank".

Jesus says, *"Until now you have not asked for anything in my name. Ask and you will receive, and your joy will be complete"* (John 16:24).

God is now your Heavenly Father. You're part of his family. You can talk to him not *just* at special times — you can talk to him throughout the day!

But don't forget to say sorry and ask for forgiveness when you mess up.

Church?
Which church?

If you don't belong to a church yet, you must think carefully about joining one as soon as possible. Christians get stronger as they worship together. Also, God uses groups of Christians to work for him. You may have heard someone describe the church as being like a bonfire! The sticks burn well when they're all together in the fire. When one is taken out, it won't burn brightly any more, and the flame may even go out. Are you "on fire" for the Lord? Then make sure you stay in the fire with other Christians!

As you look around, you'll see different churches. Some have been built specially as churches, and others will be small halls, or even people's homes. You'll see different names for these churches. There will be Baptist, Brethren, Church of England, Methodist, Pentecostal, United Reformed — and many others. These are "denominations".

Each denomination will be different from the others: perhaps in the type of Sunday Service, or in the way the church is run. Some denominations have their own minister (or vicar or pastor), while others have a group of elders who invite different people to preach each Sunday.

There are big differences between some denominations, and it would be silly to pretend there weren't. Sometimes these differences cause unpleasant arguments, and this is a great shame when there are so many things they *can* agree on. Of course, in many towns groups of Christian churches work together. These are exciting times for young Christians, and you will be able to share in this "coming together" of so many different churches.

Probably no one wants all churches to be exactly the same. Some people like a noisy service with worship songs they can clap their hands to. Others like a very quiet time of worship. I'm talking here about "ordinary" Christian churches.

Be warned. There are some groups that may call themselves Christian, but they don't teach that Jesus is the Son of God, or that he died to forgive our sins as a free gift. Among these are Christadelphians, Christian Scientists, Jehovah's Witnesses (with the Watchtower magazine), Mormons (Latter Day Saints), Spiritualists, and groups that take young people away from their families. Jesus warned that in the last days (the time near his return):

"False Christs and false prophets will appear and perform signs and miracles to deceive the elect — if that were possible. So be on your guard; I have told you everything ahead of time" (Mark 13:22-23).

If you avoid these groups, they won't be able to lead you astray. The Lord loves you, and will keep you close to him. Here is a promise from Jesus:

"My sheep listen to my voice; I know them, and they follow me. I give them eternal life, and they shall never perish; no one can snatch them out of my hand" (John 10:27-28).

You may decide to try a few churches before you find one you want to stay with. If you live in a city the choice will be greater. If you can, find one where you feel welcome, where there are plenty of other young people with a good study or worship group for your age. Most importantly, make sure you get teaching about Jesus and the Bible.

If you find no one you know at church, invite someone to go with you. Some churches have a family service either every week or once a month. Perhaps a parent or friend would go with you, even if they don't go already. Later, the Lord may lead you to a church where you can help it "come alive". Right now, look for a church with a service that you can enjoy. Yes, it *is* possible to enjoy going to church! But even more important than that — and this really is important — remember, you need a church that teaches the Bible.

Let us not give up meeting together, as some are in the habit of doing, but let us encourage one another — and all the more as you see the Day approaching (Hebrews 10:25).

The Day mentioned here is the time when Jesus will return to take all his followers — including you if he returns in your lifetime — to be with him in heaven for eternity.

One very important step to take soon in church is to be baptized, if you've not been baptized already. Ask your church minister or leader for guidance on this.

Christian books are a great way to find out more about the Lord and grow in the Christian faith. Again, ask your church minister or leader for help. The internet is full of unhelpful teaching, and is *not* the way to learn about God and the Bible.

The enemy

It won't be long before you become aware that God has an enemy. We mentioned him earlier. Probably you've encountered him already. Right from the beginning, Satan, the devil, has been making trouble. However, the devil is not a powerful god — he's nothing more than a fallen angel, with fallen angel followers. But he can cause a lot of problems. Yes, some people laugh at the idea of a devil because all they think of are cartoons where he's seen with horns and a tail. Other people get so worried about him that they're paralysed with fear. Please don't fall into either of these traps.

> Jesus says, "*I have told you these things, so that in me you may have peace. In this world you will have trouble. But take heart! I have overcome the world*" (John 16:33).

> Paul writes, *Finally, be strong in the Lord and in his mighty power. Put on the full armour of God so that you can take your stand against the devil's schemes* (Ephesians 6:10-11).

Paul goes on to tell us more about the armour of God — the belt of truth, the breastplate of righteousness, the shield of faith, and so on in this chapter of Ephesians. Please read about it for yourself. Paul was writing to Christians, so we certainly need to take note, but not of course be obsessed about the devil. However, an enemy wants nothing better than for people to think that he doesn't exist, or that there is no danger, so they stop being watchful.

How do we keep out of danger? First, remember that the Christian life can be dangerous at times, and keeping out of danger might involve choosing to go back to your old way of life — and surely you wouldn't want to do that.

Of course, not everything that goes wrong is caused by the devil. We can do some pretty stupid and nasty things by ourselves, without any help from outside. But the devil hates God, and he therefore hates all Christians.

Who do you think it is who says to you, "Go on, it won't *really* matter if you do that." And afterwards says, "Call yourself a Christian, when you behave like that!" It's a trap. Don't fall into it.

So what can we do about him? Daily prayer, daily Bible reading, living openly as a Christian, worshipping with other Christians, support from a Christian friend. Well, you get the idea. All these will help keep the enemy away. And if he's leaving you alone completely, perhaps he's decided that you're not much of a threat to his kingdom. Live the Christian life to the full. That way, *you* will be the threat to *him*, and of course you will have God on your side. Never let yourself be defeated.

Be the picture on the left, not the one on the right. But fight in the strength of the Lord God, not in your own strength. It's the armour of *God*! Read Ephesians chapter 6 again.

"EXCUSE me, but . . . !

Perhaps you feel now that you would like to tell someone that you've become a Christian, if you haven't done it already. Telling someone (perhaps another Christian) will do you good. Afterwards, you'll somehow feel more sure in your own mind what has happened to you. There's another good reason for telling other people — you may be able to help *them* become Christians.

> So do not be ashamed to testify about our Lord, or ashamed of me his prisoner. But join with me in suffering for the gospel, by the power of God (2 Timothy 1:8).

Paul was in prison for his faith when he wrote this letter to Timothy. Now, how do you tell someone you're a Christian? First of all, pray. Ask Jesus to choose someone for you to tell. If you keep going up to strangers and saying, "Excuse me, but...!" you'll probably end up making a nuisance of yourself and get nowhere — although some people do have a definite gift from God to do this. And you may be one of them.

Did someone help *you* to become a Christian by talking to you? If so, you can be sure the Lord led them to speak to you —

even though they may not have realized it at the time. Only the Lord knows how ready someone is to receive him. He knew *you* were!

Telling another Christian should not be difficult, because you'll find it easy to explain to them what's happened to you. If the person you're telling is *not* a Christian, remember that *your* words only get as far as their head. It is the Lord who speaks to their heart. No clever argument from you will *make* them become a Christian. Say what has happened to you and what Jesus means to you. Keep it simple.

> *In your hearts set apart Christ as Lord. Always be prepared to give an answer to everyone who asks you to give the reason for the hope that you have. But do this with gentleness and respect* (1 Peter 3:15).

If you've asked the Lord to help you share your new faith, be ready for that prayer to be answered! Copy some verses into the back of your Bible or into this book. Here are some you may find useful if someone wants to know more. Up to now, the words of each verse have been written out for you. If you're interested in helping your friends find Jesus for themselves, you'll be prepared to look these up now — and learn them!

> *Romans 3:23; Romans 6:23; Acts 16:.31; John 14:6; Ephesians 2:8-9; 1 Corinthians 15:3-4; Revelation 3:20; 2 Corinthians 5:17; 1 John 1:9; 2 Peter 3:18; John 1:12.*

Your friend *may* be ready right then to pray a prayer that will make the Lord Jesus Christ their Saviour. You can copy out the prayer on page 4 of this book into the back of your Bible along with these verses. Never, ever force someone into praying this prayer if they're not ready to really mean it. When you're ready to tell someone about Jesus, you may be "sowing seed". In months or even years they may remember what you told them and come to accept the Lord Jesus Christ, even if you're not there.

Don't be disappointed if you seem to get nowhere. If it's someone in your family or a friend you've been talking to, you *must keep on* praying for them.

What you do is often as important as what you say. Can your family see a difference in you since you became a Christian? Or are you the same old cross, thoughtless, selfish, unloving person you always were?!!! Well, you probably weren't all *that* bad, but can you see the point?

Whatever you've done that's wrong, try to put things right — even if it means there could be problems for you. If knowing Jesus seems to make so little difference to you that you keep quiet about it, why should anybody else be interested in knowing him? Is it time to unzip those lips?

Where now?

Maybe you lack the confidence to believe deep down that God the Father Almighty, Creator of heaven and earth, really loves you. You still think of yourself as a sinner, a miserable maggot. If this is so, why did God bother sending his Son Jesus Christ to pay for your forgiveness? You're not a sinner anymore — you're a saint! That's how the New Testament describes Christians. People are sinners *before* they become Christians. They are called saints afterwards — although we are of course saints who still sin and need to ask for the forgiveness that God *promises*.

If this is so, why should we bother about how we live our new lives? Here are two verses from the NIV, and on the next page are the same verses from the two translations mentioned at the start of this book. They are from 2 Timothy 2:20-21. There is no suggestion here that one version is somehow more "holy" than another. They are simply different in their choice of some English words in their translation from the original Hebrew and Greek.

In a large house there are articles not only of gold and silver, but also of wood and clay; some are for noble purposes and some for ignoble. If a man cleanses himself from the latter, he will be an instrument for noble purposes, made holy, useful to the Master and prepared to do any good work. (NIV)

But in a great house there are not only vessels of gold and of silver, but also of wood and of earth; and some to honour, and some to dishonour. If a man therefore purge himself from these, he shall be a vessel unto honour, sanctified, and meet for the master's use, and prepared unto every good work. (KJV)

In a well-furnished kitchen there are not only crystal goblets and silver platters, but waste cans and compost buckets — some containers used to serve fine meals, others to take out the garbage. Become the kind of container God can use to present any and every kind of gift to his guests for their blessing. (TMG)

So it looks like we all have a choice about what sort of Christian lives we live, about whether we are useful to God or not!

 Finally . . .

There is always something new to discover in the Christian life, and this book has done little more than touch the surface. Lots more could be said, but now we come to our final pages ...

The Christian life is not easy all the time. Even the greatest Christians have had problems:

I do not understand what I do. For what I want to do I do not do, but what I hate I do (Romans 7:15).

This was written by one of the greatest Christians in the Bible — Paul. If he couldn't do any better, what hope do we have! But don't give up. To begin with, it really is quite something to *know* what is right, and *want* to do it. And it isn't just *you* doing the wanting anyway. Paul knew a way out of the difficulty. Here it is:

For it is God who works in you to will and to act according to his good purpose (Philippians 2:13).

If God is helping you, that's much better than trying to manage by yourself. Paul says in 2 Corinthians 5:17:

Therefore, if anyone is in Christ, he is a new creation; the old has gone, the new has come!

So, made all new, in a new family — God's. God has a plan for your life. Keep close to him, and make sure you ...

... Cast all your anxiety on him because he cares for you (1 Peter 5:7).

Jesus said to his disciples:

"Therefore go and make disciples of all nations, baptizing them in the name of the Father and of the Son and of the Holy Spirit, and teaching them to obey everything I have commanded you. And surely I am with you always, to the very end of the age" (Matthew 28:19-20).

Is Jesus saying something like this to you today? Many Christians hear his call. You don't have to wait for a few years. The disciples started straight away — in their own towns!

TAKE A LITTLE TIME NOW TO THANK YOUR HEAVENLY FATHER FOR ANYTHING HE HAS BEEN SPEAKING TO YOU ABOUT WHILE READING THIS BOOK, AND ASK HIM TO HELP YOU TAKE HIS WORDS FROM YOUR HEAD TO YOUR HEART.

USE THESE BLANK PAGES TO MAKE NOTES, AND COPY OUT SOME BIBLE VERSES THAT NOW MEAN A LOT TO YOU. COME BACK HERE REGULARLY OVER THE NEXT YEAR OR TWO, READ WHAT YOU'VE WRITTEN, AND ADD TO IT. (MORE PAGES AT THE BACK.)

"Can I know I'm a Christian and going to heaven?"
"I'm definitely a Christian, but now I seem to be stuck. Why?"
"I used to believe, but what's happened to the faith I once had?"

Do you sometimes ask yourself one of these questions? If you do, you're not alone. Even if you don't have any uncertainties in your own faith, maybe you know someone you can help.

Whether this book is for you, or you're reading it to help a friend, it provides some commonsense advice on living a fuller and more confident life in Jesus Christ, no matter how badly things have been going up to now.

HELP!
Published by White Tree Publishing
Paperback ISBN: 978-0-9927642-2-7
38 pages
Also available as an e-Book ISBN: 978-0-9933941-1-9

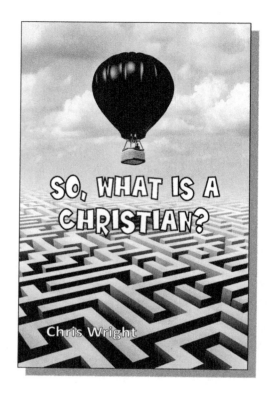

So, What Is a Christian? is another book by Chris Wright, published by White Tree as a companion to *Starting Out* and *Help!* The same size as *Starting Out* and *Help!* it explains what a Christian really is and tells the reader the steps to becoming part of God's family.

SO WHAT IS A CHRISTIAN?
Published by White Tree Publishing
Paperback ISBN 978-0-9927642-3-4
38 pages
Also available as an e-Book ISBN: 978-0-9933941-2-6

Not sure how the Bible fits together? Abraham and Moses? The Exodus and the Exile? Confused over kings and prophets? Old Testament, New Testament? We'll start at zero, and assume nothing. We're running through the Bible in only 38 pages, and we won't be travelling alone. There's a red cord running with us, starting in Genesis where we begin our journey, through to Revelation at the end. The red cord binds the Bible together. It's God's rescue plan for the people he created, giving us a way out of the mess we've made of our lives through the free will he has given us.

RUNNING THROUGH THE BIBLE
Published by White Tree Publishing
Paperback ISBN: 978-0-9927642-6-5
38 Pages
Also available as an e-Book ISBN: 978-0-9933941-3-3

Printed in Great Britain
by Amazon

21044565R10031